Weather

Written by Sally Morgan

Wayland

Bodies   Fairgrounds   Light   Special Days
Boxes   Growth   Patterns   Textures
Changes   Holes   Rubbish   Weather
Colours   Journeys   Senses   Wheels

Picture acknowledgements

The publishers would like to thank the following for allowing their photographs to be reproduced in this book: ECOSCENE 7 (below/Greenwood), 8 (Glover), 9 (below/Hibbert), 10, 11 (above/Glover), 11 (below/Gryniewicz), 14 (Glover), 15 (below/Cooper), 17 (above/Morgan), 19 (Meech), 20 (above/Brown), 20 (below/Beatty), 21 (Hawkes), 23 (Morgan), 24 (above/Brown), 24 (below/Cooper), 26 (Morgan), 27 (above/Whittle), 28; Tizzie Knowles 29 (above); Oxford Scientific Films Ltd 13 (Warren Faidley), 15 (above/Ronald Toms), 17 (below/Richard Packwood), 18 (Hans Reinhard), 22 (Ronald Toms); Tony Stone Worldwide 4 (above/David Sutherland), 6 (Jo Browne/Mick Smee), 7 (above/David Sutherland), 16, 27 (below); ZEFA 4 (below), 5, 9 (above), 12 (above), 25 (both), 29 (below).

**Cover and title page photography by Daniel Pangbourne,
organized by Zoë Hargreaves.
With thanks to the Fox Primary School.
A special thank you to Hebe and Charlie.**

First published in 1993 by
Wayland (Publishers) Ltd
61 Western Road, Hove
East Sussex BN3 1JD, England

© Copyright 1993 Wayland (Publishers) Ltd

Editor: Francesca Motisi
Designers: Jean and Robert Wheeler

Consultant: Alison Watkins is an experienced teacher with a special interest in language and reading. She has been a class teacher but at present is the special needs coordinator for a school in Hackney. Alison wrote the notes for parents and teachers and provided the topic web.

British Library Cataloguing in Publication Data
Morgan Sally.
Weather – (Criss Cross Series)
I. Title II. Series
551.6

ISBN 0-7502-0766-3

Typeset by DJS Fotoset Ltd, Brighton, Sussex
Printed and bound in Italy by L.E.G.O. S.p.A., Vicenza

Contents

Words that appear in **bold** in the text are explained in the glossary on page 32.

All sorts of weather

The weather can be hot or cold, cloudy or sunny, dry or wet. What is the weather like today?

Weather affects us in many different ways.
It affects the clothes we wear, the food we eat
and the sports we play.

Sunny days

Sunny days make us feel happy, cheerful and warm. The sky is blue and there are few clouds. We wear less clothes so that we stay cool.

These children are enjoying the sunny weather on a beach.

Animals like the sun too. This butterfly has opened its wings to warm them in the sun.

Windy weather

A gentle breeze blows a sailing boat
slowly through the water.

A stronger wind keeps kites up in the air.

Winds that are even stronger are called gales and they can blow the leaves off trees. The strongest winds are called hurricanes. They are strong enough to cause a lot of damage.

9

Clouds

Clouds are made from millions of tiny drops of water. The many different shapes of clouds can tell us a lot about the weather. Fluffy white clouds are called cumulus clouds. They tell us that the weather will be fine.

Thin, wispy clouds are a sign of good weather too. They are called cirrus clouds.

But if the clouds join together to form a thick, dark layer across the sky, then there may be rain.

Storms and rain

Dark clouds produce rain. When it rains, we wear waterproof clothes or put up an umbrella so that we stay dry.

If it is raining and the sun is still shining, you may be lucky enough to see a rainbow. This one is in Australia.

Thunderstorms can be frightening. Bright flashes of **lightning** light up the sky, followed by a boom of **thunder**.

Too much rain

Some countries like Indonesia have very heavy rain. The houses are built on stilts to keep above the **flooded** ground.

If there is a lot of rain a river can fill up with water and burst over its banks. Fields of crops may disappear under the water.

Areas in towns can be flooded too, like this playground. It's too wet to play in now!

Too little rain

When it does not rain for a long time rivers, lakes and ponds dry up. Animals and plants cannot get enough water to drink and farmers' crops may die. In some parts of the world, it may rain just once or twice a year. These places are called deserts.

Very few plants or
animals can live in
deserts. But one
type of plant, the
cactus, can live
for a long time
without water.
Its thick stems
can store water
until it rains again.

When rain does
fall in a desert it
is soon a mass
of flowers.

17

Dew and mist

Spiders' webs and grass are often damp with dew early in the morning. Dew is made of tiny drops of water. It forms when the water in warm air meets the cooler surface of the blades of grass and changes into water droplets. It quickly disappears when the sun comes out.

Mist is a very thin cloud that can be seen in valleys and woods in the morning. Just like the dew, it soon goes when the sun shines on it.

Fog

Fog is thick cloud
that forms near
the ground.
The bridge in this
photograph is
almost hidden
by fog.

Fog can be dangerous because you cannot see through it. Many car accidents happen in fog because the drivers cannot see the cars in front of them.

Frosty weather

On cold nights in winter, feathery patterns of ice appear on windows and over the ground. You wake up in the morning to a **landscape** of frosty, ice-covered land.

Frost covers the leaves of plants. It sparkles in the sun, but melts as soon as the **temperature** rises above **freezing**.

Snow

Snow is frozen water that falls from the clouds. Snowflakes slowly flutter to the ground, covering the ground in a soft, white blanket.

The snow has to be cleared away when it covers our roads and paths.

Snow can be fun.
What do you like
to do in the snow?

◀ Snowflakes come
in many different
shapes, but they
all have six points.

Hot and cold places

The type of weather in a place is called its **climate**. Some places near the **Equator** have a hot and wet climate all year. Rainforests grow here.

The coldest parts of the world are the North and South Poles. The ground is covered in a thick layer of snow and ice that never melts.
The animals have to live in the terrible cold.

Penguins have feathers to keep them warm.

Polar bears have thick coats of fur and a layer of fat to help them ▶ stay warm.

Tomorrow's weather

There are some simple ways of telling if the weather will change. A red sunset often means that the next day will be fine. There is an old saying: *Red sky at night, shepherd's delight.*

28

Pine cones can tell you if it is going to rain. If you put a pine cone outside and its scales open up, the weather will probably be dry. But if it closes them, it will probably rain.

Today people use modern machines to find out what the weather will be like.

Notes for parents and teachers

Science
● To show how plants use sunlight to help them grow and keep healthy, plant a seedling in a pot. Put it on the window-sill and watch it grow towards the light. What happens when it is put in a dark corner?
● Hot air rises and cooler air moves into its place. This happens in the atmosphere. If you hold your hand over a radiator you can feel the hot air rising. It is lighter than the cold air and so rises above it.
● To understand condensation put a glass of iced water in a warm room and water will condense on the cold glass.
● Evaporation is when water disappears into the air. Hang out two wet cloths, one where it is sunny and one in the shade. Which dries first?
● Make a list in your home or school of the things which are affected by the sun.

Language
● Use alliteration in story and poetry writing e.g. wild winter winds, pitter patter etc.
● Make an information book about cold or sunny lands of our world.
● Write an adventure story and include as many different types of weather as you can.
● Suitable fiction:
   Mog in the fog by H. Nicoll and J. Pienkowski, (Puffin, 1984).
   The Day of the Rainbow by R. Craft, (Little Mammoth, 1988).
   The Weather Cat by H. Creswell and B. Walker, (Collins, 1989).
   The Bears' Winter House by J. Yeoman and Q. Blake, (Macmillan, 1987.)

Maths
● A maths topic on Time and Seasons would help the children develop their understanding of this concept. Children can use measurement in real and practical tasks. They can also record results or outcomes of events. Through this topic children should be encouraged to understand, estimate and calculate probabilities.

Technology
● Children can plan, design and make different instruments for measuring the weather. They can describe how they made it and how it works.

Art/Crafts
● Children can mix paints to create sunset colours. Then using black card they can cut out trees, birds or roof-top shapes and stick them on to the background.
● Paint a large wall frieze showing the different activities we do in the different seasons.

Dance/Drama
● Use the story of the wind and the sun as a stimulus for movement. Basically it is an argument between the two over who is the strongest.
● Children can make up a short play about a day out at the seaside. They can think about the props they would need.

Music
● Listen to various pieces of music and imagine the different types of weather it conveys (e.g. Vivaldi's *Four Seasons*).
● Learn songs and rhymes about the weather, e.g. *The Rainbow Song, Dr Foster went to Gloucester, Rain Rain Go Away* etc . . .

R.E.
● Discuss with the children how the failure of eagerly awaited rainstorms can trigger widespread drought. This causes loss of crops and famine the following year in developing countries. Flooding can also ruin crops and have the same results.

History/Geography
● Children need to understand that weather is very important to all of us. It affects what we wear, what kind of food we eat, what kind of home we live in and how we spend our time.
● Farmers throughout the world are dependent on the weather for the success or failure of their harvest.
● To help understand the water cycle, watch a kettle boiling. Heat makes the water in the kettle turn to steam. The steam escapes and looks like a little cloud. When the steam touches the window it condenses and changes back into drops of water because the glass is cool.
● Find out about how the Inuit live today in comparison with how they used to live.

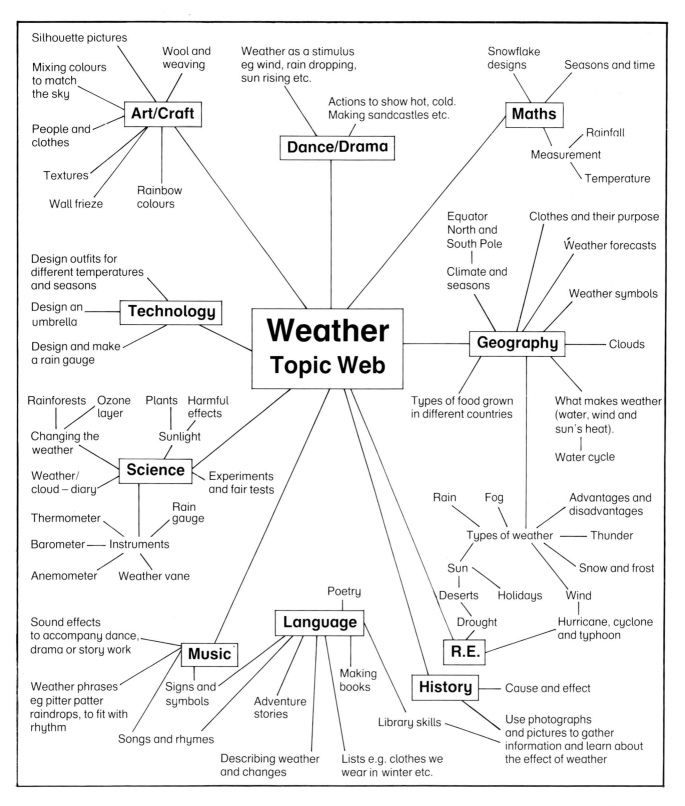

Weather
Topic Web

Art/Craft
Silhouette pictures
Wool and weaving
Mixing colours to match the sky
People and clothes
Textures
Wall frieze
Rainbow colours

Dance/Drama
Weather as a stimulus eg wind, rain dropping, sun rising etc.
Actions to show hot, cold. Making sandcastles etc.

Maths
Snowflake designs
Seasons and time
Rainfall
Measurement
Temperature

Technology
Design outfits for different temperatures and seasons
Design an umbrella
Design and make a rain gauge

Geography
Equator North and South Pole
Climate and seasons
Clothes and their purpose
Weather forecasts
Weather symbols
Clouds
Types of food grown in different countries
What makes weather (water, wind and sun's heat).
Water cycle

Science
Rainforests
Ozone layer
Plants
Harmful effects
Changing the weather
Sunlight
Weather/cloud – diary
Experiments and fair tests
Thermometer
Rain gauge
Barometer — Instruments
Anemometer
Weather vane

Music
Sound effects to accompany dance, drama or story work
Weather phrases eg pitter patter raindrops, to fit with rhythm
Signs and symbols
Songs and rhymes

Language
Poetry
Making books
Adventure stories
Describing weather and changes
Lists e.g. clothes we wear in winter etc.
Library skills

R.E.
Types of weather
Rain
Fog
Advantages and disadvantages
Thunder
Sun
Holidays
Snow and frost
Deserts
Wind
Drought
Hurricane, cyclone and typhoon

History
Cause and effect
Use photographs and pictures to gather information and learn about the effect of weather

Glossary

Climate   The type and pattern of weather in a place or country.

Equator   An imaginary line around the centre of the Earth.

Flooded   If land is flooded, it is covered with water. This is usually caused by heavy rainfall.

Freezing   Very cold, a temperature of 0°C.

Landscape   The view you can see all around you.

Lightning   An electric flash in the sky seen during thunderstorms.

Temperature   How hot or cold it is.

Thunder   Thunder is the loud noise heard in a storm. It usually follows lightning because sound travels more slowly than light.

Index